Where's the Gift?

How to achieve phenomenal success by
discovering the gift in *all* feedback

Nigel
Bristow

The author can be contacted at Targeted Learning:
    722 E. Heather Road
    Orem, UT 84097
    Tel: 801-235-9414
    Fax: 801-235-9424
    email: nigel@targetedlearning.com

Volume discounts are available on this and other publications by Nigel Bristow. Details can be found on page 78.

ISBN 1-57636-090-3

Printed in the United States of America
at Cascade Press in Lindon, Utah

Cover design—Stacy Keith
Layout—Alana Lee
Illustrations—Patrick Bristow and Jackie Hickman
Editorial and production support—Lori Jacobson

Where's the Gift?
Table of Contents

This book is dedicated to all those people who have given me feedback to raise my standards, as well as my spirits.

Introduction

Can you think of any skill you possess that you acquired without the benefit of some type of feedback? Probably not. The reality is, learning is impossible without feedback. In learning to walk, talk, read, and write, feedback was essential to your success.

Because feedback ensures learning, and learning determines our success in life, feedback is one of the greatest gifts that one person can offer another. Whether the feedback comes in the form of a gentle reminder or a harsh rebuke, it represents a gift—if you know how to find it. This book will teach you how to accelerate your learning and maximize your success by finding the gifts in all forms of feedback.

"Honest criticism is hard to take,
particularly from a relative, a friend,
an acquaintance, or a stranger."

~Franklin P. Jones

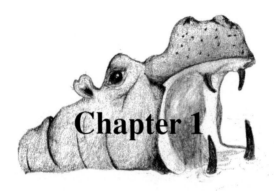

Why the Hippo Spends His Days in the Water

"You won't believe what just happened to me!" exclaimed Matt, as he stormed into his mentor's office. "That Jalee is the most sarcastic supervisor I've ever had. It's not just that she's always on my case; I could probably handle that if she didn't have the interpersonal skills of a chainsaw!"

"It sounds like your meeting was brutal," said Paula. "What happened?"

It took Matt several minutes before he could calmly give Paula the details of the meeting. Matt liked being able to talk about his work problems with Paula, his mentor for the past six months. She gave little advice but was a great listener. And by talking openly about his problems, Matt often discovered his own solutions. But this time it was different. After fifteen minutes, Matt was still clueless about how he should deal with his interpersonally-challenged supervisor.

"Matt," offered Paula, "I've got to go to a meeting, so I can't continue our discussion right now. But I have an old African folktale that I'd like you to read and think about. If possible, let's meet tomorrow morning at 7:30 for breakfast in the cafeteria. Then we can talk some more. Will that work for you?"

After giving her protégé the African folktale, Paula left for her meeting. As soon as Matt got back to his desk, he started to read.

Why the Hippo Spends His Days in the Water

The first hippopotamus to walk the earth had a beautiful fur coat and a thick mane that was rivaled only by that of the lion. Although his coat had been given to him by Nature, Hippo took full credit for its beauty, and loved to show it off whenever he could. Hippo did not like the night because its darkness hid his coat from the other animals.

With his fine fur coat, Hippo didn't need to sleep near the fire. His coat gave him plenty of warmth. But over time, Hippo started to sleep closer and closer to the fire. He did this so that the light from the fire would allow his coat to be seen by the other animals throughout the night. Lion gently warned Hippo not to sleep so close to the fire, but Hippo dismissed Lion's warning by saying, "Lion is just jealous because all the animals can see both day and night that my coat is better than his."

Jackal was also worried about the safety of Hippo, but Jackal, despite her great intellect, found it difficult to be tactful. "You great hairy oaf," said Jackal. "Your inflated pride is only matched by your girth. Your pride is going to get you into trouble one of these nights."

Hippo was indignant. "How dare she speak to me like that. When she learns to treat me with respect, then I'll listen. Who asked for her opinion anyway?"

One night, as I'm sure you've already guessed, Hippo got too close to the fire and his beautiful fur coat caught fire. Hippo made a desperate dash for the river, but by the time he dived into the water, it was too late. His beautiful fur coat had gone up in smoke.

At about sunrise, Hippo had cooled off sufficiently to leave the river. But when he looked down into the water, he saw in his reflection that his beautiful fur coat was gone. His ugly rough skin was exposed for all the animals to see. "If only I had listened to Lion and Jackal," thought Hippo. He then dived back into the water.

To this day, in order to hide his embarrassment, Hippo spends the daylight hours concealed in the water of the river. He only ventures out of his watery hiding place at night so he can eat without worrying about who might see his ugly skin.

The next day Matt and Paula met as planned for breakfast in the cafeteria. "Now that you've had a chance to read the folktale and think about your experience with your boss, what do you think?" asked Paula.

"I think," replied Matt, "that the African folktale was your way of giving me feedback. And I've got to tell you, it stung! Yesterday my complaints about my supervisor's feedback sounded so reasonable when I uttered them. Yet when the hippo said something similar, it sounded somewhat self-defeating."

"What sounded self-defeating?" asked Paula.

"Like when the hippo complained that the jackal wasn't respectful in the way she gave him feedback," replied Matt. "Maybe I'm a little like the hippo. On the other hand, Jalee's supposed to be my supervisor. The company talks about people being important, and they even have 'respect for the individual' written in the company's values statement. Surely Jalee ought to know how to give better feedback."

"Maybe she should," agreed Paula. "But she obviously doesn't, so you're going to have to figure out a way around that. When I started at this company, my first supervisor taught me to think of feedback as a gift. And whenever I'd complain about a less than tactful customer or colleague, he'd say, 'Now don't throw the gift away because you don't like the wrapping.' Do you see anything like that happening with Jalee?"

"Definitely," admitted Matt. "I can't see the gift because of the atrocious wrapping."

"So you're going to have to keep reminding yourself that there's a gift hidden in there somewhere. And if you do, you'll invariably find it. But how about the lion in the story? When I first read the story, it struck me that Hippo rejected Lion's warnings for reasons other than the wrapping. Did you see any parallels between that part of the story and feedback in the workplace?" asked Paula.

Matt quickly scanned the story. "Not at the time," acknowledged Matt. "But now that I've looked at it again, it seems to get more personal with the lion. With the lion, the problem was not the wrapping but the messenger. Hippo saw Lion as a competitor, and an inferior one at that. So he was suspicious of Lion's motives and rejected the message. But, I don't think that's a problem I have with Jalee. With Jalee, it's the wrapping thing."

"I think you're right," said Paula. "The reason I raised it was not because of the problem you're having with Jalee. Rather, it's just something for you to keep in mind down the road when you get feedback from people you're not sure you can fully trust—or people who perhaps aren't as talented as you, but might still have a perspective you could learn from."

"That makes sense," agreed Matt. "So I guess the two messages from the parable are: Don't throw the gift away because of the wrapping, and don't reject the message just because you don't like or respect the messenger."

"Right. And one last thing," observed Paula. "When I was asked to be a mentor in the company, I was cautioned that my role was not to put into the protégé what nature left out, but to bring out more of what nature had put in. And that's what I would suggest you do with your supervisor."

"I'm not sure I know what you mean," offered Matt.

"Think of it this way. What did nature leave out of your supervisor? What are her weaknesses?" asked Paula.

"Interpersonal stuff. Communication," replied Matt.

"And what did nature put in?" asked Paula. "What are her strengths?"

"Well, I guess she has good analytical skills and a keen eye for potential problems," acknowledged Matt a little grudgingly.

"Okay, Matt. So what I'm suggesting is that you look beyond what nature left out of Jalee, and try to focus on what nature gave her."

"So what you're saying is, instead of wishing that she were more personable, I should work harder to benefit from her analytical gifts. That's going to be tough, but it's worth a try."

"Good luck. Let me know how it goes with Jalee—or anyone else, for that matter," said Paula.

After returning to his office, Matt wrote the following in his learning journal.

- *Feedback is a gift.*
- *Don't discard the gift of feedback just because you don't like the wrapping.*
- *Don't reject the gift simply because you don't like or respect the giver—or because you suspect his/her motives.*
- *Don't just look for what you want; look for what the other person has the ability to give.*

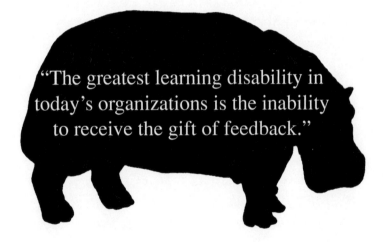

"The greatest learning disability in today's organizations is the inability to receive the gift of feedback."

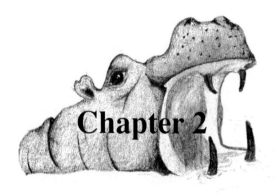

The Gift

A few days later, Matt ran into Paula in the cafeteria. "Matt, if you have a minute, I have a gift in my office that I'd like to give you."

"You mean you want to give me some feedback?" Matt asked with a smile.

"Not at all," said Paula as they walked back to her office. "But you responded so well to the hippo story that I thought you might appreciate this particular gift."

"I have a question for you," asked Matt. "What if the person giving you feedback is basing it on faulty information? Isn't it dangerous to take every piece of feedback at face value and just act upon it?"

"It could be very dangerous," replied Paula. "You should seldom, if ever, take feedback at face value. Sometimes it will be inaccurate. Sometimes the person giving it will be out of touch with your unique situation. But that doesn't mean it can't be of value to you. Let me share a personal example. A few years ago, I got feedback from someone in another group. He told me I was failing to meet my commitments, which was clearly false. I mean, I had met every commitment he referred to. And I had the reports to prove it. But I still learned a valuable lesson from the feedback."

"What was the lesson?" asked Matt.

"Well," continued Paula, "the learning came from trying to figure out how this person reached his ill-informed conclusion. I realized that while I was meeting my commitments, I was not keeping the right people informed. So I started to communicate more deliberately with more people, and it's made a huge difference to my career. So you could say that one of the most helpful pieces of feedback I ever received was based on faulty information. Quite the paradox, isn't it?"

When they entered Paula's office, Matt immediately saw a large box on Paula's desk. The box stood about eighteen inches high. It was wrapped in plain brown paper with Matt's name scribbled on the top. "I don't know what's in here," said Matt as he moved the box to the edge of the table, "but thank you. I can't wait to see what you've put in here for me."

Matt opened the lid of the box and started to remove packaging materials made out of shredded paper. After removing five inches of shredded newspaper, Matt found a shoebox. He pulled it out and opened it, only to find more shredded newspaper. After taking a moment to offer a smile and a shrug in Paula's direction, Matt resumed the search. Eventually, with shredded newspaper almost covering the top of Paula's desk, Matt found the gift. It was a beautiful small hippo carved out of wood.

"Thanks, Paula. This little hippo is great," said Matt with a broad smile. "I'm going to keep it on my desk to remind me of the hippo's folly."

"Now," said Paula, "you probably noticed that there was a metaphor within the metaphor."

"Yes," replied Matt. "I did notice that the wrapping was somewhat scrappy—a reminder that helpful feedback doesn't always come in a neat package with a pretty ribbon tied around it."

"Excellent," noted Paula. "Anything else?"

"Well," offered Matt, "as I rummaged through all of the shredded paper I kept asking myself 'Where's the gift?' I must have asked myself that question at least half a dozen times before I eventually found the carving. So I guess it's a pretty good question to ask myself whenever Jalee gives me her less than tactful feedback."

"Correct, and there's even more than that," prompted Paula. "Take some time today and think through the steps people go through when they receive a gift—the very same steps you went through when I gave you the box and told you there was a gift inside. Then relate those steps to the process of receiving the gift of feedback."

Later that same day, after describing the events surrounding the hippo carving to a friend, Matt thought carefully about the experience of receiving the wooden hippo. He compared it to experiences where he had received helpful feedback in the past, pulled out the similarities, and identified four steps. After rewriting the four steps several times, Matt transcribed them into his learning journal:

__Four Steps to Receiving the Gift of Feedback__
1. Acknowledge the Gift.
— Say "thank you."
*— Assume that you're about to discover
   something of value.*
2. Open the Box and Seek the Gift.
*— Sometimes the gift is hard to find in
   the packaging material.*
*— To find the gift, ask lots of questions
   and really listen with an open mind.*
*3. Acknowledge the Nature and the
   Value of the Gift Inside.*
*— Put into words what you understand
   the gift to be (summarize).*
*— Mention how you plan to use it (if
   you can at this point).*
4. Use the Gift.
*— When you use it and experience the
   benefits of the gift, let the giver know
   how it has helped you.*

Matt then amended the first principle he had written down a few days earlier. Instead of just leaving it as "Feedback is a gift," he extended it to read:

- *Feedback is a gift—even when it may be inaccurate.*

Finally Matt added another principle:

- *Ask yourself the question, "Where's the gift?" And continue to ask that question until you find the gift.*

"Most people would rather be ruined by praise than honored by criticism."

—Norman Vincent Peale

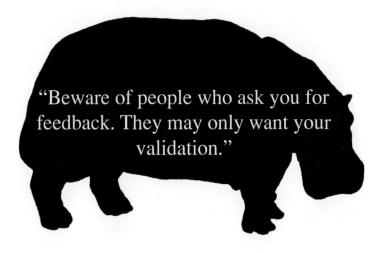

"Beware of people who ask you for feedback. They may only want your validation."

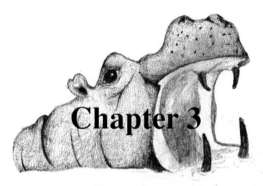

Back on the Farm

A few weeks later, Matt and Paula met in the cafeteria for their monthly lunch-time discussion.

"You know, Paula, your guidance on treating feedback as a gift has been invaluable. I took your advice and created a four-step process for receiving feedback, and I've been using it with Jalee. It's remarkable how much I've been able to learn from her in the last couple of weeks. Whenever she gives me feedback that is obscured by sarcasm or generalizations, I think of it as a game. I win the game whenever I find the gift that is hidden in her message. So far I'm five for five."

"So," asked Paula, "how do you play the game?"

Matt handed Paula a typed copy of the four-step process before proceeding. "I start with a simple 'Thanks for bringing this to my attention.' Then I say something like, 'I'd really like to understand this'—and then I ask some questions and listen as carefully as I can. I find it a lot easier to listen openly when I keep asking myself questions like 'Where's the gift?', and 'What can I learn from this.' When I think I've found the gift, I summarize what I've gleaned from the discussion and ask if I've missed anything. So far it's worked like a charm."

"Great. And how has it affected your relationship with Jalee?" asked Paula.

"I'm not sure, but I think I've already noticed an improvement in the quality of her feedback. Now that she knows I take her feedback seriously, she seems to be giving it with less intensity and more clarity," answered Matt.

"That sounds like real progress," said Paula. "Just give me a few moments to read through your four-step model."

Four Steps to Receiving the Gift of Feedback
1. *Acknowledge the Gift.*
— *Say "thank you."*
— *Assume that you're about to discover something of value.*
2. *Open the Box and Seek the Gift.*
— *Sometimes the gift is hard to find in the packaging material.*
— *To find the gift, ask lots of questions and really listen with an open mind.*
3. *Acknowledge the Nature and the Value of the Gift Inside.*
— *Put into words what you understand the gift to be (summarize).*
— *Mention how you plan to use it (if you can at this point).*
4. *Use the Gift.*
— *When you use it and experience the benefits of the gift, let the giver know how it has helped you.*

"Matt," said Paula enthusiastically, "this model of yours is excellent! There are two pieces you captured that I've never explicitly thought about before—the part in Step 3 about mentioning how you plan to use the feedback, and then later in Step 4, telling the person how it's helped you. Those steps should really keep the door open for more feedback in the future."

"I'm glad you like it," said Matt. "I've got to confess that when I started to write some ideas down, I wasn't too confident it would yield very much. But by the time I finished it, I felt really good about it. By the way, any thoughts on how I might improve on it?" asked Matt.

"Nothing big," answered Paula. "The only thing I'd add is something at the end of Step 2. I'd add a point about never explaining yourself, because the moment you start explaining, you stop learning. And to make matters worse, even the most legitimate explanation will usually come across as an excuse. It makes you appear defensive."

Four Steps to Receiving the Gift of Feedback

1. Acknowledge the Gift.

— *Say "thank you."*

— *Assume that you're about to discover something of value.*

2. Open the Box and Seek the Gift.

— *Sometimes the gift is hard to find in the packaging material.*

— *To find the gift, ask lots of questions and really listen with an open mind.*

3. Acknowledge the Nature and the Value of the Gift Inside.

— *Put into words what you understand the gift to be (summarize).*

— *Mention how you plan to use it (if you can at this point).*

4. Use the Gift.

— *When you use it and experience the benefits of the gift, let the giver know how it has helped you.*

"I never thought of that," said Matt. "But it makes a lot of sense. Thanks, Paula."

"Now, there's something I'm struggling with," admitted Matt. "I've become so convinced that feedback is a gift that I'm now asking people other than Jalee for feedback. But all I get from a lot of people is, 'Hey, you're doing a good job. Just keep doing what you've been doing.' What can I do if people are reluctant to give me feedback?"

"Why do you think they're reluctant?" asked Paula, pushing Matt to think more critically.

"Well," answered Matt, "I think most people don't like conflict, and consequently they avoid saying anything critical. They're pretty much the opposite of Jalee. I used to think Jalee's feedback was unhelpful. Now I'm beginning to believe that the most unhelpful feedback is no feedback at all."

"I think it always helps to be explicit about why
you want the feedback and how you plan to use
it," said Paula. "And while that will work with a
lot of people, others will need a little prodding.
Here's a principle I learned from my grandfather.
We visited his farm most summers. He had no
running water in his house, but relied on a manual
water pump just outside the kitchen door. One
morning, he asked me to go out and pump water
into a bowl he had given me. I came back and told
him the pump was obviously broken because no
matter how hard I pumped, I couldn't get any
water. He laughed and told me that a pump is like
anything else in life—if you want anything out of
it, you have to first put something in. He promptly
picked up a bucket of water that stood next to the
pump, and poured a little water into the pump.
Then he asked me to try again. This time the water
flowed. He called that procedure 'priming the
pump.' If you want honest feedback from some
people, you may first have to prime the pump with
a little self-critique. So let's say you wanted to
prime the pump in the area of improving your
facilitation skills. How would you do it?"

"Well," said Matt hesitatingly, "I guess I could start by saying something like: 'I'm working on improving my meeting facilitation skills. One thing I think I could improve on is getting team members more involved, umm, ...perhaps by asking more questions and then giving them more time to respond. What else do you think I could do to improve my facilitation skills?' ...So Paula, is that what you mean by priming the pump?"

"I couldn't have modeled it better myself," smiled Paula. "While lots of people ask others for feedback, the reality is that many of those who ask for feedback are just fishing for validation. When you prime the pump, you reassure the other person that you genuinely want to improve...that you're not just looking for validation."

"Okay, here's another problem I've noticed," said Matt. "Sometimes when I ask for feedback, people get into areas that are no longer relevant to what I'm doing or to the type of projects I'm now working on. What can I do about that?"

"How have you asked for feedback?" asked Paula.

Matt responded, "Basically, I just say, 'I'm putting together a development plan and I would really appreciate it if you could help me by giving me some honest feedback....' OK, now I see it. You think I need to be more specific about the feedback I want, right?"

"Exactly," confirmed Paula. "So you'd say something like, 'I'm working on my presentation skills and since you've been at two of my most recent presentations, I was hoping you could give me some ideas for improvement.'"

"Okay, then," said Matt. "One more question. What should I do when they give me feedback on my presentation skills, and there is some feedback that I disagree with? If I honestly think that what they're suggesting will make matters worse rather than better, what should I do then?"

"Is that before or after you've gone through the process of asking questions about their ideas and summarized your understanding of their ideas?" asked Paula.

"Afterwards," said Matt.

"What do your instincts tell you?" asked Paula.

"I think I'd take what I can use and set the rest aside," replied Matt.

"As long as you've honestly sought to understand their feedback, then that makes perfect sense. Remember, feedback is simply information you use to steer your life in the direction of your goals. If you think their suggestion will take you in the wrong direction, then you have to weigh the evidence and do whatever your best judgement tells you. I've got to admit that sometimes I get a gift from my mother I can't use. But I never toss it back at her and say, 'Thanks, Mom, but I really don't want it.' That would probably hurt her feelings, particularly since she always taught me that 'it's the thought that counts.' So I take it and thank her for her thoughtfulness. And it's not necessary for me to fake that, because I know her intent was to give me something of value. Then I put the gift on a shelf in the hopes that I'll find a good use for it down the road. Sometimes I do, and sometimes I don't. But I never do anything to suggest that I don't appreciate her efforts."

Later that day, Matt added the following to the list in his journal:

- *The most unhelpful feedback is no feedback.*
- *When asking for feedback, be explicit about what you want and why you want it.*
- *When asking for feedback, be ready to prime the pump with a self-critique.*
- *Learning from feedback doesn't require you to do exactly what others tell you. But it does require you to listen, and to understand what they're saying and why.*

Matt then added two more items to his four-step model:

<u>Four Steps to Receiving the Gift of Feedback</u>

1. Acknowledge the Gift.
— Say "thank you."
— Assume that you're about to discover something of value.
2. Open the Box and Seek the Gift.
— Sometimes the gift is hard to find in the packaging material.
— To find the gift, ask lots of questions and really listen with an open mind.
— *Never explain yourself.*
3. Acknowledge the Nature and the Value of the Gift Inside.
— Put into words what you understand the gift to be (summarize).
— Mention how you plan to use it (if you can at this point).
4. Use the Gift.
— When you use it and experience the benefits of the gift, let the giver know how it has helped you.
— *When you can't use the gift immediately, simply say "thank you" and put it on a shelf until you discover a use for it.*

"Take each man's censure but reserve thy judgement."

—Shakespeare in *Hamlet*

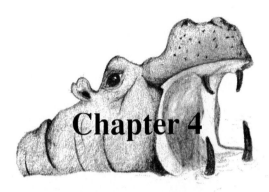

But What if You Have to Explain Yourself?

At their next monthly lunch, Matt discussed with Paula a few of the challenges he was facing on some of his projects. They explored some strategies for dealing with the barriers, and then the discussion shifted back to the topic of feedback.

"I'm very pleased with how the four-step process and priming the pump have worked for me," said Matt. "What's most remarkable is how my supervisor's behavior around giving feedback has changed. By changing how I receive her feedback, I appear to have changed how she gives me feedback—and it's all for the better. But I've got to confess that yesterday I was in a situation where the four steps just didn't seem appropriate."

"What happened?" queried Paula.

"Jim, from the accounting department, came over and told me I had gone over my budget. That was totally incorrect. I know I shouldn't have tried to explain myself, but if I hadn't, he could have interpreted my open acceptance of his feedback as an admission of guilt. Not only would that be misleading, but it could hurt me if he started taking his incorrect information to higher levels."

"So what did you say?" asked Paula.

"Well," responded Matt, "I immediately tried to explain the facts of the situation. But I'm not sure it did any good."

"Why not?" prompted Paula.

"Because he wasn't listening. He seemed to just block it out and kept saying he had the figures in black and white, so I just needed to face reality," complained Matt.

"Okay, Matt. Now I want you to put yourself in Jim's shoes for a minute," suggested Paula. "When he has to go and tell someone that they've overspent and he's going to shut down their account, what do you think his experience has taught him?"

"To get ready for a battle," responded Matt.

"Exactly," confirmed Paula. "When the Roman Legions went to war they not only took their offensive weapons such as spears or swords, but they also expected to get some resistance, so they took their shields too. Now when Jim comes in with his numbers, he knows he's likely to be in a battle, so he has his psychological shield at the ready. When you tell him he's wrong and pull out evidence to prove it, guess what he sees?"

"A sword?" answered Matt.

"Right. So what does he do with his shield?" asked Paula.

"He defends himself with it," answered Matt.

"Precisely. He holds up his shield to deflect your blows. Consequently, Matt, your explanations buy you nothing. The trick is not to simply explain yourself. The trick is to be heard," explained Paula.

"But how do I get through his shield so that I can be heard?" asked Matt.

"For starters, you can't go through the shield. You've got to make it safe enough for him to put his shield down. Which of the four steps of your model are critical to making the other person feel respected and safe?" asked Paula.

Matt thought for a few moments. "Well…, I think the first three steps would all help."

"So tell me Matt, which steps did you neglect when you immediately defended yourself against his unfair and misinformed feedback?" asked Paula.

Matt nodded. "All of the above. I never even got to the point of asking myself 'Where's the gift?' or 'What can I learn from this?'" After a prolonged pause Matt continued, "So what you're saying is that I should follow the first three steps, and then when he puts his shield down, I hit him with my sword?"

Both Matt and Paula laughed. "Not quite," offered Paula, "but you're close. You summarize the feedback and ask, 'Have I captured it accurately?' If he says 'no,' then you ask a few more questions to clarify, and you summarize again. Once he confirms to you that you've understood him completely, then you offer your side of the story."

<u>Four Steps to Receiving the Gift of Feedback</u>

1. Acknowledge the Gift.
— Say "thank you."
— Assume that you're about to discover something of value.

2. Open the Box and Seek the Gift.
— Sometimes the gift is hard to find in the packaging material.
— To find the gift, ask lots of questions and really listen with an open mind.
— *Never explain yourself.*

3. Acknowledge the Nature and the Value of the Gift Inside.
— Put into words what you understand the gift to be (summarize).
— Mention how you plan to use it (if you can at this point).

4. Use the Gift.
— When you use it and experience the benefits of the gift, let the giver know how it has helped you.
— *When you can't use the gift immediately, simply say "thank you" and put it on a shelf until you discover a use for it.*

"But what if he still refuses to listen?" asked Matt.

"That's not likely to happen. Most people are fair-minded, and when you make a sincere and explicit attempt to understand them, they invariably reciprocate by listening to you," reassured Paula.

"But Paula, what if they're not fair-minded?" asked Matt with a hint of a whine in his voice.

"Well, you've lost nothing—because the other person wouldn't have listened to your explanations anyway," replied Paula. "But you may still have gained something that might be very valuable to you in the future."

"What's that?" asked Matt.

"By asking the questions and listening," explained Paula, "you gain a clearer understanding of the other person's information and concerns. That means that if he won't listen to you and the two of you don't resolve your differences, then you've gained the advantage by becoming much better informed. If the issue now has to be resolved at a higher level, you're better equipped to persuasively present your case. I know that some people find this almost impossible to do. They feel that by doing all the listening, they're allowing the other person to score all the points and get the advantage. The paradox is that the harder you try to win the argument, the greater the likelihood that you're going to fail. Listening is the most effective tool for getting your message across"

"I see your point," acknowledged Matt. "So whether they're fair-minded or not, it's to your advantage to go all the way through the first three steps *before* trying to explain yourself."

"Exactly! And here's an additional strategy that will sometimes be very appropriate," suggested Paula. "It's especially important when the situation is emotionally charged or if you firmly believe the other person is being unfair. After Step 1, 2, or 3, take a time-out. That gives both of you some time to get past the emotions. This also allows you to gather some data, think through what you have been told, and decide what an appropriate response may be. Consequently, you're less likely to respond defensively, or to respond in a way that might lead the other person to raise the shields. So a day or two later, or as soon as you've worked through your own emotions and are ready to talk, you go back and restart the conversation by thanking the other person for bringing the information to your attention. But one word of caution, Matt. Don't defer the conversation as a way to avoid dealing with a tough issue."

"I agree. But what if it's an urgent issue that needs to be dealt with immediately?" asked Matt.

"If that's the case, then you obviously have to explain yourself—there and then," confirmed Paula. "But only do it when you're sure you understand the other person—*and* when they confirm that you understand. On the other hand, when you do have the luxury of time, and can defer your response until later, you'll be amazed at how much more effective your response will be."

Matt nodded. "You know, perhaps I need to try this with Jim. At this point I've got nothing to lose."

"So what will you say?" prompted Paula.

"I guess I should probably start with an apology for getting defensive," answered Matt. "Then I'll tell him that since our last conversation, I've spent a lot of time trying to get things clear in my mind. I'll tell him it's an important issue for me to understand, and I'll ask him if he'd mind helping me. Then I'll summarize my understanding of his feedback and concerns, and ask if I've got it right. Once he confirms I've understood him, I guess I've earned the right to tell him about anything I think he's missed."

"Excellent," said Paula. "So I guess my earlier
statement about never explaining yourself was
wrong. At the end of Step 2, it should say: 'Don't
explain yourself—at least not until after Step 3,
when you understand the feedback and the giver
believes you understand.'"

At this point, Paula altered what was written in
Step 2 of Matt's four-step process.

Four Steps to Receiving the Gift of Feedback

1. Acknowledge the Gift.
— Say "thank you."
— Assume that you're about to discover something of value.
2. Open the Box and Seek the Gift.
— Sometimes the gift is hard to find in the packaging material.
— To find the gift, ask lots of questions and really listen with an open mind.
— ~~Never~~ *Don't* explain yourself—*at least not until after Step 3, when you understand the feedback and the giver believes you understand.*
3. Acknowledge the Nature and the Value of the Gift Inside.
— Put into words what you understand the gift to be (summarize).
— Mention how you plan to use it (if you can at this point).
4. Use the Gift.
— When you use it and experience the benefits of the gift, let the giver know how it has helped you.
— When you can't use the gift immediately, simply say "thank you" and put it on a shelf until you discover a use for it.

Matt leaned forward. "You know, it's just dawned on me how critical that first step is, particularly the piece about assuming you're about to find something of value. Because if you think there's a bomb in the package, you're never going to take the risk of opening it. You won't even get beyond Step 1. But when you assume they truly are giving you a gift, then finding the gift is a lot easier."

"Now you've got it," said Paula. "You always give the giver the benefit of the doubt. It's a lot like forgiveness. When one person forgives another, it's usually the person doing the forgiving that stands to gain the most. So when you assume that the feedback giver truly wants to give you something of value, you make that assumption as much—or even more—for your own benefit as for theirs."

"Well, I think I'm ready to handle Jim's feedback about the budget in a more constructive way," said Matt. "Thanks for your help. I'll let you know how it goes."

When Matt got back to his office, he updated his four-step process by adding a statement to the end of Step 3. It said: *"If appropriate, share your feelings or views (but only if you can do so without coming across as defensive)."* Matt then added three more principles to his list:

- *If you want to be heard, make it safe for the other person to lay down the shield.*
- *Take a time-out if you need time to think through what you've been told, or time to get your defensiveness under control.*
- *When you assume that the feedback giver wants to give you something of value, you make that assumption as much (or even more) for your own benefit as for theirs.*

The next morning, having thought deeply about how he should approach Jim, Matt visited him in his office.

"Jim," said Matt, "I'd like to apologize about my reaction to your feedback yesterday. I'm really sorry I got defensive. I know you were only doing your job of managing our budgets. So if now's a good time, I'd like to understand your numbers a little more and clarify the next steps we need to take."

"Now's as good a time as any," replied Jim. "Here's the issue...."

Matt followed the steps very carefully. He had even scripted out some of the things he wanted to say and the questions he needed to ask. As Jim responded to Matt's questions, Matt continued to ask himself "Where's the gift?" and "What can I learn from this?" Within ten minutes, the shields were down, and Matt was able to explain his side of the story. Within another five minutes, they had resolved the issue and cleared up the misunderstandings on both sides.

By following this process, Matt gained an important insight. By going through the first three steps, he not only created an environment where Jim felt safe to listen, he also discovered where his own information and assumptions were off the mark. Matt added one more principle to his list:

- *When you're convinced that the other person is misinformed, remain open to the possibility that you might also be misinformed.*

"Excuses—don't use them. Your friends don't need them and your enemies won't believe them."

—Unknown

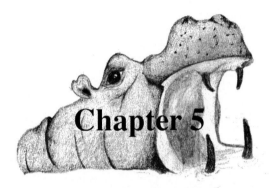

A Few Years Later

Paula took a promotion in another part of the company, and Matt moved ahead in his own career. Matt quickly distinguished himself through his own work accomplishments, and in time he was asked to be a mentor.

Beth, Matt's new protégé, was sitting in his office waiting for him when he got to work.

"Matt," Beth began, "there's something I need your help with. My supervisor, Kathy, rarely gives me feedback. But when she does, it's like a big data dump—and often it's so late that there's nothing I can do with it. I know that the supervisor's job is to give helpful feedback to subordinates. I just don't know if I trust her to be able to give me good feedback."

"Well," suggested Matt, "let's start with what has happened. Take a few minutes and tell me about some of your experiences with feedback from Kathy, and how you responded to it."

As Beth described her experiences, Matt started to take notes and draw a little diagram. "Don't worry," he reassured Beth. "I'm only summarizing what you've experienced so we can both look at the dynamics from a different angle. So keep sharing—it'll help me capture the process more accurately."

Throughout the discussion, Matt asked questions to clarify and probe for more details. When Matt felt that he understood the situation, he pushed his sketch towards Beth and said, "Now take a look at this cycle. Does it capture what's happening?"

A Vicious Feedback Cycle

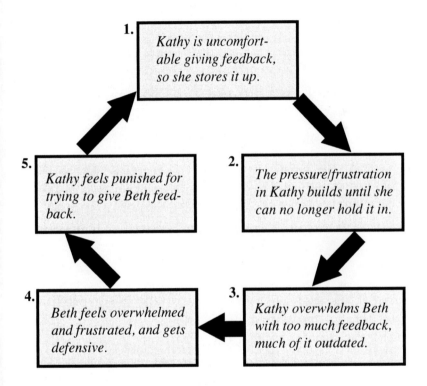

1. *Kathy is uncomfortable giving feedback, so she stores it up.*

2. *The pressure/frustration in Kathy builds until she can no longer hold it in.*

3. *Kathy overwhelms Beth with too much feedback, much of it outdated.*

4. *Beth feels overwhelmed and frustrated, and gets defensive.*

5. *Kathy feels punished for trying to give Beth feedback.*

After a few moments, Beth looked up. "This is scary. I never saw it this clearly before, but it seems to sum up the dynamics incredibly well."

"And who is feeding the vicious cycle?" asked Matt.

"Both of us," replied Beth.

"Now that you've seen the cycle, who's in the best position to break it?" asked Matt.

"I suppose I am . . . because at least I now recognize what's happening. But she's the boss, which means she has more power to change it," complained Beth.

"It may be true that she's got more formal power. But what's the likelihood she'll use it to change the situation?" asked Matt.

After a brief pause, Beth responded with a faint smile of resignation on her face. "I guess I've got to face reality. If this cycle is going to change, I'm going to have to make the first move."

"So how do you plan to do that?" probed Matt.

Beth answered by thinking out loud. "Somehow I've got to help her see that giving feedback can be a positive experience. But first I've got to get over my own knee-jerk defensiveness. Although in all honesty, that's often triggered by the fact that she tries to give me too much too late."

"So what can you do to help Beth get into the habit of giving more regular feedback?" prompted Matt.

"I guess what I really need to do first is ask her for feedback on a more regular basis, rather than waiting for her to give it to me. And then I need to make sure I treat it as if I truly value it, regardless of what she says," answered Beth.

"I think that's a great idea," confirmed Matt. He then gave Beth a few ideas on how to ask for specific feedback, and how to "prime the pump," if necessary. At the end of their conversation, as Beth was about to leave his office, Matt encouraged her to let him know the outcome of her first self-initiated feedback conversation with Kathy.

Matt reflected on his discussion with Beth. It had been a few years since he had updated the list of principles for receiving feedback in his learning journal. The nice thing about being a mentor, he thought to himself, is that you can sometimes learn a lot from your protégé. He took the list out and added one more principle:

- ***The quality of the feedback we get often depends more on our skill at receiving it than on the skill of the person giving it.***

Looking at his list, Matt marveled at how his career had been transformed by applying these principles. He reorganized his learnings under four headings:

- *Realities about Feedback*
- *Principles for Seeking Feedback*
- *Principles for Receiving Feedback*
- *Four Steps to Receiving the Gift of Feedback*

Realities about Feedback

- Feedback is a gift—even when it may be inaccurate.
- The most unhelpful feedback is no feedback.
- The quality of the feedback we get often depends more on our skill at receiving it than on the skill of the person giving it.
- Learning from feedback doesn't require us to do exactly what others tell us. But it does require us to listen, and to understand what they're saying and why.
- When you assume that the feedback giver wants to give you something of value, you make that assumption as much (or even more) for your own benefit as for theirs.

Principles for Seeking Feedback

- When asking for feedback, be explicit about what you want and why you want it.
- When asking for feedback, be ready to "prime the pump" with a self-critique.

Principles for Receiving Feedback

- Treat feedback as if it were a gift.
- Don't discard the gift of feedback just because you don't like the wrapping.
- Don't reject the gift simply because you don't like or respect the giver—or because you suspect his/her motives.
- Don't just look for what you want; look for what the other person has the ability to give.
- Take a time-out if you need time to think through what you've been told, or time to get your defensiveness under control.
- If you want to be heard, make it safe for the other person to lay down the shield.
- When you're convinced the other person is misinformed, remain open to the possibility that you might also be misinformed.
- Ask yourself the question, "Where's the gift?" And continue to ask the question until you find the gift.

Four Steps to Receiving the Gift of Feedback

1. Acknowledge the Gift.
— Say "thank you."
— Assume that you're about to discover something of value.

2. Open the Box and Seek the Gift.
— Sometimes the gift is hard to find in the packaging material.
— To find the gift, ask lots of questions and really listen with an open mind.
— Don't explain yourself—at least not until after Step 3 when you understand the feedback and the giver believes you understand.

3. Acknowledge the Nature and the Value of the Gift Inside.
— Put into words what you understand the gift to be (summarize).
— Mention how you plan to use it (if you can at this point).
— If appropriate, share your feelings or views (but only if you can do so without coming across as defensive).

4. Use the Gift.
— When you use it and experience the benefits of the gift, let the giver know how it has helped you.
— If you can't use the gift immediately, simply say "thank you" and put it on a shelf until you discover a use for it.

Matt decided he ought to write a short book about receiving feedback. He grabbed his keyboard and created the title:

Where's the Gift?

I listen to critics because often they're a good source of information for what you have to do differently.

John Chambers, President of CISCO

Sharing the Gift With Others

If you wish to share your learnings from this book
with others, details for ordering additional copies
can be found on pages 78-79. In the interim, the
best way you can share these lessons is to put them
into practice in your own life. The appendix
contains tools to help you do this.

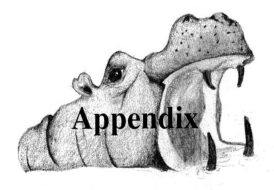

Moving to Action

Now that you know why all feedback is a gift, and how to receive it as a gift, it's time to act.

Part A: Selecting Those You Should Ask

You should seek feedback from anyone who has insights about either you or your work. Select someone you trust, whose perspectives will help you learn about yourself and your growth opportunities:

❐ manager/supervisor   ❐ spouse
❐ customers   ❐ children
❐ business partners   ❐ parents
❐ manager's manager   ❐ friends
❐ direct reports   ❐ teachers
❐ peers or colleagues   ❐ coaches
❐ team members   ❐ mentors
❐ family   ❐ other(s)

List the names of at least five potential feedback givers:

_____   _____

_____   _____

_____   _____

_____   _____

_____   _____

Part B: Deciding When to Ask

Effective feedback is ongoing. It should become a part of your personal continuous improvement program. Here are some occasions when you may wish to seek feedback:

- At key milestones or the completion of projects.
- When the comments or body language of others suggest that they have concerns.
- When you have concerns about your impact on others or about your performance.
- Prior to, during, and after team meetings, presentations, etc.
- When there is a change in job expectations or customer commitments.
- When you are looking for new growth opportunities.
- When you need a sounding-board for your ideas or proposals.

Identify <u>at least two</u> people who could give you helpful feedback right now:

_____   _____

_____   _____

Part C: Preparing to Receive Feedback

This exercise will help you prepare to receive feedback.

<u>Who</u>—Identify one person from whom you'd like to receive feedback as soon as possible:

_____

<u>When</u>—When will you ask for this feedback? (Identify a specific time or situation.)

_____

<u>How</u>—(Be prepared, be specific.)

1. What do you want feedback about? Be specific!_____

_____

2. Why do you need this feedback? How will it help you? _____

_____

3. How will you state your request? Be specific.

_____

_____

_____

4. Is this person likely to resist giving you frank feedback? If yes, how might you overcome this resistance? (For example, what self-critique could you use to "prime the pump?")

_____

_____

Part D: Asking For It

Remember to apply the first three steps of the
Model for Receiving the Gift of Feedback:

1. Ask for and acknowledge the gift.
    —Explain what you need feedback on and why.
    —Say "Thank you."
2. Open the box and seek the gift.
    —Ask questions.
    —Listen.
    —Don't explain.
3. Acknowledge the nature and value of the gift.
    —Summarize your learnings.
    —Mention how you'll use it .
    —If appropriate, share your views.

Part E: Using the Gift

Complete this exercise *after* you have received
your feedback.

1. What did you learn about the process of
   receiving feedback? _____

   _____

   _____

2. What did you learn from the content of the
   feedback itself? _____

   _____

   _____

3. What should you do based on the feedback you
   received? _____

   _____

   _____

4. Who can help you clarify the feedback or
   support you in your efforts to grow from the
   feedback? How? _____

   _____

   _____

5. When you've gained the benefit, *be sure to let
   the giver know how it helped you.*

Other Learning Resources from Nigel Bristow and Targeted Learning

Share the Gift with Others

Volume Pricing on Books

Title	Pricing
1. *Where's the Gift?* How to achieve phenomenal success by discovering the gift in *all* feedback	1-4 @ $15.95 5-20 @ $13.95 21-50 @ $11.95 51+ @ $9.95
2. *Flying the Coop*: Liberating ourselves from the mindsets that limit our potential and rob us of fulfillment	1-4 @ $17.95 5-20 @ $15.95 21-50 @ $13.95 51+ @ $11.95
3. *Strategies for Career Success:* Principles and tools for building career vitality and resilience	1-10 @ $35.00 11-25 @ $30.00 26 + @ $25.00
4. *Building Communities of Learning:* How to harness the collective genius of the people in your organization	1-10 @ $25.00 11-25 @ $22.50 26 + @ $20.00
5. *The New Leadership Imperative:* How to transform knowledge workers into STARS	1-25 @ $10.00 26-50 @ $9.00 51 + @ $8.00
6. *Using Your HR Systems to Build Intellectual Capital and Organization Success*	1-25 @ $10.00 26-50 @ $9.00 51 + @ $8.00

Shipping Information:

For Ground Shipping
- Orders will be shipped ground unless otherwise requested (allow 5-10 business days).
- $5.00 for small orders (up to 4 items).
- $1.00 for each additional book, not to exceed $15.00.

For Express Delivery
- Overnight or 2 to 3 day shipments will be billed at cost.

Order Form

Titles	Quantity @ $	Total
1. *Where's the Gift?*	@ $	
2. *Flying the Coop*	@ $	
3. *Strategies for Career Success*	@ $	
4. *Building Communities of Learning*	@ $	
5. *The New Leadership Imperative*	@ $	
6. *Using Your HR Systems*	@ $	

Name: _____ **Shipping** _____

Title: _____ **Total $** _____

Company: _____

Address: _____

City: _____ State: _____ Zip: _____

Phone #: _____ Fax #: _____

Payment Method:

☐ Check (please include with order—payable to Targeted Learning)

☐ Credit Card #: _____ Exp. Date: _____

Name on card: _____

☐ AMEX   ☐ Visa   ☐ Mastercard

For credit card purchases:
- call us at (801) 235-9414
- or complete this form and fax it to us at (801)235-9424
- or complete the form and mail it to the address below

For purchases by check:
- please complete and mail this form along with your check to the address below

Targeted Learning, 722 East Heather Road, Orem, UT 84097

Related Products and Services from Targeted Learning

Other products and services that help individuals maximize their learning and performance:

❑ **Seeking and Receiving the Gift** *(2 hours or 1/2 day)*
A workshop that teaches participants how to get timely, honest, face-to-face feedback that will maximize their growth and performance.

❑ **Giving the Gift** *(2 hours or 1/2 day)*
A workshop that teaches participants how to give feedback to others that will promote confidence, growth, and performance.

❑ **Receiving and Giving the Gift** *(1/2 day or 1 day)*
A workshop to help individuals and teams achieve excellence by harnessing the full power of feedback.

❑ **Career Leadership Skills** *(1 or 2 days)*
A workshop that helps individuals take charge of their growth and performance in today's flatter, more fluid organizations. Participants learn how to target those learning opportunities that will maximize their productivity, career satisfaction, and employability.

❑ **Coaching for Superior Performance** *(1/2 day, 1 day, or 2 days)*
A workshop designed for those who must help others grow and succeed in today's less hierarchical organizations. Participants learn how to unleash the potential of others and create a climate that fosters learning, innovation, and superior performance.

❑ **Quickstart for Protégés** *(1 day)*
A workshop that helps new employees quickly become highly-valued contributors to their teams and organizations. Participants learn how to leverage the mentor-protégé relationship for personal, team, and organizational success.

❑ **Mentoring Skills for Professionals** *(1 or 2 days)*
A workshop that equips individuals with the skills they need in order to share their knowledge and help others succeed.

❑ **Consulting Resources**
We are experts in the systems and processes required to support effective career development, performance leadership, knowledge leadership, and customer-inspired innovation.

Information Request Form

Please check the boxes below to request information on our training and/or consulting resources:

❑ Seeking and Receiving the Gift
❑ Giving the Gift
❑ Receiving and Giving the Gift
❑ Career Leadership Skills
❑ Coaching for Superior Performance
❑ Quickstart for Protégés
❑ Mentoring Skills for Professionals
❑ Consulting Resources

Name _____ Title _____

Organization _____

Address _____

Phone # _____ Fax # _____

E-mail _____

Fax this completed page to (801) 235-9424, **OR**

Call us to request the information at (801) 235-9414, **OR**

E-mail us—data@targetedlearning.com (include your name, organization name, title, complete address, phone and fax numbers).

For more immediate information about Targeted Learning, **visit our website** at www.targetedlearning.com

Ideas for using
Where's the Gift?

This book was originally written as a self-help tool for people who wanted to exercise more control over their own learning. Targeted Learning clients, however, have found additional ways to use the book and its message. Here are some ideas:

♦ **Marketing Organization:** As prereading for a team building session.

♦ **Aerospace Company:** As reading for all protégés enrolled in a formal mentoring program.

♦ **High-Tech Company:** As the basis for a module on feedback in a workshop on career management skills.

♦ **Manufacturing Company:** As the foundation for a stand-alone workshop on seeking, receiving, and giving feedback.

♦ **R&D Organization:** As reading to prepare employees for their annual performance reviews (to set a tone of openness and non-defensiveness).

♦ **Financial Services Company:** As a take-home resource for participants in a mentoring skills workshop.

♦ **Bio-Tech Company:** As a self-study resource for the launch of a new performance management system.